the Classical Piano

THE INFLUENCE OF SOCIETY, STYLE, AND MUSICAL TRENDS ON THE GREAT PIANO COMPOSERS

Includes Full-Length Piano Solos and Complete Performances on 2 CDs

SELECTED, EDITED, AND ANNOTATED BY NANCY BACHUS
PERFORMED BY CONCERT PIANIST DANIEL GLOVER

Cover Design: Sunny Haihua Yang
Interior Design: Tom Gerou
Music Engraving: Bruce Nelson and Greg Plumblee
Supervising Editor: Sharon Aaronson

Cover art:
George, 3rd Earl Cowper, with the family of Charles Gore, ca. 1775
by Johann Zoffany (1733–1810)
Oil on canvas
Yale Center for British Art, Paul Mellon Collection, USA
Photo Credit/Bridgeman Art Library

D1294985

Contents

Track Listing and Music Pages

Foreword

To understand and interpret musical style, it is necessary to capture the spirit of the time in which the composers lived, created, and performed. Classical musical style developed around the mid-18th century in Europe as composers relied less on patrons and began writing in a newer, simpler style for a public wanting music for entertainment and personal music making. During the Classical era, the piano, invented around 1700, edged out the harpsichord as the favorite keyboard instrument. Instruction books from the time give insight into performing the music, with one stating that all tones (not slurred) must be cleanly separated.[1] There is also an admonition that the beginning of each slur group should have a gentle emphasis, and lifts occur only at the end of the large musical phrase.[2]

Nancy Bachus's *The Classical Piano* brings this era alive by integrating music with other fields of knowledge—social and political events, scientific achievements, and trends in art and architecture. This book combines historical paintings, notable quotations, and information about composers with full-length, original pieces and 2 CDs containing performances of all the works.

Artistically performed by concert pianist Daniel Glover, the CDs serve to motivate piano practice as a model for performance as well as to provide listening enjoyment. These pieces of various moods, tempos, forms, and styles may be studied in any order.

Part 1 of this volume explores the background of the Classical era—events and trends that influenced Classical musical life. Part 2 focuses on the greatest composers of the day along with the sonata cycle and commonly used forms. *The Classical Piano* is certain to be an indispensable resource and personal treasure for all music lovers.

NANCY BACHUS taught both applied piano and academic subjects for more than 25 years at the college and university levels. A graduate of the Eastman School of Music, where she studied with pianist Eugene List and accompanist Brooks Smith, she was one of the performers in the original "Monster Concerts" in New York City (Radio City, Lincoln Center, Carnegie Hall) and the White House. She has been a featured clinician for numerous piano teachers' organizations throughout the United States, Canada, England, Scotland, and Southeast Asia. Certified as a Master Teacher by the Music Teachers National Association (MTNA), Nancy currently maintains an independent piano studio in Hudson, Ohio.

DANIEL GLOVER has performed in 42 states and 22 countries throughout North America, the Caribbean, Europe, and Asia. A graduate of the Juilliard School, where he was a scholarship student, he has trained with Eugene List, Abbey Simon, Jerome Lowenthal, Nancy Bachus, and Thomas LaRatta. Performances include a successful Carnegie Hall recital in 1992, a result of winning the Artist's International Competition, as well as appearances in Washington, D.C.'s Corcoran Gallery, and the St. Petersburg Palaces Festival in Russia. A reviewer wrote, "He is a master of intricate detail, and can produce truly magical sounds full of exciting energy."

[1] Daniel Gottlob Türk, *Clavierschule (The School of Keyboard Playing)*, trans., intro. and notes by Raymond H. Haggh (Lincoln: University of Nebraska Press, 1982), 324.
[2] Ibid., 329.

Part 1

The Influence of Classical Society, Style, and Musical Trends

Classic, Classical and Classicism

Classic, classical and classicism, in the strictest sense, refer to the language, art and culture of the **ancient Greeks and Romans**. More broadly, these terms refer to any style or creative work with characteristics derived from them. The ancient Greeks tried to understand human beings' roles in the world, their actions and values. Their conclusions became the basis for thinking about many issues in Western civilization.

In Greece, a man's knowledge of music often determined his rank in society and nobility. Slaves were prohibited from its practice. **Music was a part of the curriculum** intended to give young men moral strength and orderly minds. Winners of musical competitions were national heroes. Greek attitudes toward music became part of the foundation for Western music, although almost none of their actual music has survived.

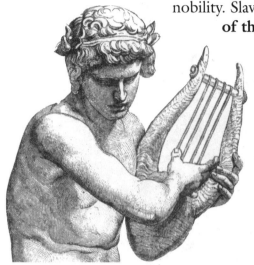

*A musician from ancient (classical) Greece playing on a **lyre**. In mythology Hermes, a messenger of the gods, made the first lyre from an empty tortoise shell.*

- Originally, the term *classicus* referred to classes in Roman society, especially to the highest class of people, things and achievements.

- Today, a **classic** is someone (or something) recognized as setting a **standard of excellence**, of high class or quality, and of enduring value. It is used to refer to art, music, literary works, fashion and sports and is associated with things that are more traditional than experimental in style.

- In a generic sense, **"classical" music** refers to all **art music** (Western music from the 15th through the 20th centuries), in contrast to **"popular" music**.

Musicians performing "classical" music

"Music has the power of producing a certain effect on the moral character of the soul, and if it has the power to do this, it is clear that the young must be directed to music and must be educated in it."

Aristotle (384–322 BC), Greek philosopher[3]

Classical Style Period (1750–1820)

The **Classical period** refers to music of the late 18th and early 19th centuries, and in the strictest sense, to the mature works of **Franz Joseph Haydn** (1732–1809), **Wolfgang Amadeus Mozart** (1756–1791), and the early works of **Ludwig van Beethoven** (1770–1827). Since they worked primarily in Vienna, Austria, Haydn, Mozart and Beethoven are known as the **Viennese Masters**. Some music historians include music by all composers from the mid-1700s to the early 1800s as part of the Classical period.

Musicians from the Classical period performing music

"Dare to know! Have courage to use your understanding! That is the motto of enlightenment."

Immanuel Kant (1724–1804), German philosopher[4]

The Enlightenment

The Enlightenment was an **intellectual movement**, begun in France in the early 1700s. Its philosophy was that the power of reason should be applied to all aspects of human life—politics, government, religion, education, the arts.

- The philosophers of this movement wanted information gathered, classified, collated and available to all. **Denis Diderot** (1713–1784) published an *Encyclopédie* between 1751 and 1772 for the purpose of *"assemble[ing] the knowledge...of the earth."*[5] They believed in humanity's natural goodness, and that conditions in society could be improved through knowledge.

- The philosophers believed the power of a monarch or government should depend upon the will of the people, with men and women free to achieve their full potential. These ideals planted the seeds for political revolution.

[3]Ian Crofton & Donald Fraser, *A Dictionary of Musical Quotations* (New York: Schirmer Books, 1985), 55.
[4]William Fleming, *Art and Ideas* (Orlando, FL: Holt, Rinehart and Winston, 1991), 421.
[5]Denis Diderot, *Encylopédie* (New York: Dover Publications, Inc., 1993, reprint), x.

Neo-Classicism in Art and Architecture

Archaeological excavations from Rome in the 1740s renewed interest in the ancient world. Eighteenth-century intellectuals idealized **Greek and Roman civilizations**.

- Ancient art (and the political ideals of republican Rome) became a model for 18th-century artists and intellectuals. Its dignity and "noble simplicity" made Rococo art appear frivolous and overdone.

- A **Neo-classic**[6] **art** emerged as buildings were designed with straight lines and geometric shapes supported by columns according to **Greek and Roman proportions**. Classical columns are common in public buildings in the Western world today.

This engraving is of the ruins of the Roman temple of Neptune. Sketched at the site by Jacques Soufflot in 1750, it was influential in the development of Neo-classic architecture throughout Europe and the United States.

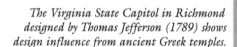

The Virginia State Capitol in Richmond designed by Thomas Jefferson (1789) shows design influence from ancient Greek temples.

The French artist, **Jacques-Louis David** (1748–1825), painted scenes from Roman history and reflected classical values in the symmetrical arrangement of figures around a focal point. On the eve of the French Revolution, there was also hidden political commentary in his paintings about current conditions in French society.

Jacques-Louis David's The Death of Socrates *(1787), points up Socrates's willingness to die for his beliefs; therefore encouraging lower-class French people to rise up against the aristocracy and, like Socrates, to make personal sacrifice, even die, for their ideals and for the greater good.*

[6] The prefix "neo" was used to describe the visual arts of this period to set them apart from antiquity. It is not necessary in the field of music since none exists from the earlier time period.

Scientific Advancement

Life was changing for individuals during the 18th century with the basics established for scientific study in medicine and other fields. Better roads, improved stagecoaches and other developments were impacting daily routines.

—**Benjamin Franklin** (1706–1790) experimented with electricity (around 1750).
—**James Watt** (1736–1819) developed a high-powered steam engine (1769).
—**James Hargreaves** (1710–1778) patented his spinning jenny (1770).
—**Joseph Priestley** (1733–1804) discovered oxygen (1774).
—**Eli Whitney** (1765–1825) invented the cotton gin (1793).
—**Edward Jenner** (1749–1823) perfected smallpox vaccinations (1796).

The Early Industrial Revolution and Its Affect on Musical Life

Scientific discoveries affected people's lives as machines and factories replaced hand tools and created new products.

- With improvements in sanitation, medicine and nutrition, the plagues and famines of the past had decreased and **population was increasing in Europe**.

- More food was produced by fewer farmers due to new methods and tools in agriculture. The beginnings of the Industrial Revolution created new service and manufacturing jobs, and **urban areas were increasing in size.**

- Improved manufacturing techniques made **musical instruments and music available and affordable** to an increasingly wealthy and powerful middle class. A public willing to pay for music lessons and concerts was developing.

An 18th-century French instrument-maker's workshop (from Diderot's Encyclopédie*).*

Trends in the Classical Period

Musical life throughout Europe at this time **reflected international culture**. Musicians traveled and **Italian** opera composers and singers, **French** dancers and dancing masters, and **German** conductors and instrumentalists were dominant in all countries.

Musicians valued qualities found in ancient art and the Enlightenment: symmetry and balance of formal design, simplicity or naturalness, and expressivity limited by the bounds of good taste.

Instrumental music surpassed vocal music in quantity and strived to be **noble** as well as **entertaining. Orchestras expanded** in size and eliminated the harpsichord. The **improved pianoforte** became the fashionable keyboard instrument of the day.

Classical Ornamentation

Classical musicians used **fewer, and less frequent ornaments** than in the recent past, and ornaments were gradually absorbed into the written score. Treatises of the time gave instruction on ornaments, but they vary on exact notation and execution. The following are generally accepted realizations of common Classical ornaments.

Any of these realizations for ornaments could vary within a specific musical context. Speed of execution depends upon the rhythm, tempo and character of the music.

Common Classical Ornaments (German Symbols)						
	Symbol	Beginning Note	Number of Notes	Direction	Rhythmic Beginning	Execution
Mordent	ꙮ	written note	3	down	on the beat	
Trill	ꙮ or *tr*	note above	4 or more depending on the length of the ornamented note	down	on the beat	
Schneller [7]	ꙮ	written note	3	up	on the beat	
Turn	∼	note above	4	down, then *turn* back up	where placed	
Trilled turn	ꙮ	note above, but it's tied	6	down, then *turn* back up	on the beat	

Long Appoggiatura: (leaning note) is played on the beat, thus delaying the principal note by half its length. If the principal note is a dotted note, the appoggiatura takes two thirds of its length.

With ordinary and dotted notes:

With a chord:

Short Appoggiatura: occurs most commonly before fast moving notes. It can be executed as a "crush," played on the beat, almost simultaneously with the principal note.

---

[7] The *Schneller* ("snap" or inverted mordent) has the same symbol as the trill. However, this ornament **begins on the main note**. It was used on fast moving notes when there was no time for a complete trill and/or to avoid striking consecutive notes in a descending line. Theorists of the time cautioned that it should not be overused.

The Classical Minuet in Various Forms

"Z" pattern of the minuet, showing pattern for dancers with verbal instructions for steps.[9]

The most popular social dance in 18th-century Europe was the **minuet**. Many **keyboard minuets** were used for actual dancing while others were **stylized**; they had characteristics of the dance, but were not intended for dancing.

Books of **choreographic notation** were published in the early 18th century describing the court dances. In the minuet, a couple moved through an elaborate floor pattern along an imaginary letter Z.[8] When they passed in the middle, they presented right hands, turned and moved to opposite corners. Next, they presented left hands, and concluded with both hands.

Presentation of the right hand in a minuet. Engraving from Kellom Tomlinson's The Art of Dancing *(18th century)*

It could take months to make these patterns appear effortless. Those who could not perform in a graceful, dignified way were considered social failures. Originally danced by only one couple, at a later time, couples danced it simultaneously, circling each other holding right hands, then left, and finally the man led with both hands.

Most minuets were 16–32 measures in length. However, according to descriptions of the time, it took 100 measures to complete the dance. Accompanying **musicians repeated sections, improvised variations,** or **performed several minuets in succession.**

Professional Women Musicians in the 18th Century

By the late 18th century, professional female musicians were **singing** in operas and court ballets, **appearing as instrumentalists** and **teaching music** to the nobility. Their most popular instruments were piano, violin, harp and guitar. A few women composed, and others were involved in music publishing and piano manufacturing.

[8]The "Z" was adapted by dancing masters from its original "S" (the sign for the Sun King, Louis XIV).
[9]Pierre Rameau, 1725.

Elisabetta de Gambarini was known in London primarily as a professional singer who performed in many of George Frideric Handel's (1685–1759) oratorios. She was also an organist, orchestral conductor and composer. This minuet is from her sixth *Sonata for Harpsichord*.

Minuet form: binary or two-part

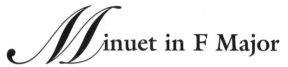

(In binary form, the first section cadences on a **V** chord.)

Minuet in F Major

Allegretto

SECTION A

Elisabetta de Gambarini
(1731–1765)

Ⓐ Throughout this book, the editor suggests that all notes not marked with a slur be played nonlegato, with a slight separation.

Johann Christoph Friedrich Bach, the oldest son of Johann Sebastian Bach (1685–1750) and Anna Magdalena Bach (1701–1760), spent most of his life as a court musician in Bückenburg, Germany.

Two Minuets

Johann Christoph Friedrich Bach
(1732–1795)

Jan Ladislav Dussek, born in Prague, was one of the first touring piano virtuosos appearing in St. Petersburg, Paris, London and many German cities. He studied with Carl Philipp Emanuel Bach (1714–1788), knew Muzio Clementi (1752–1832) and Franz Joseph Haydn, and was one of the first to produce a "singing tone" on the piano. His works were popular in his lifetime.

Minuet with Variation

Jan Ladislav Dussek
(1760–1812)

VARIATION

The Enlightenment in the United States of America

The American **Declaration of Independence** (1776) was an example of reasoned, classical thought. Instead of emotionally shouting, "Kill the King," the political leaders were logical, restrained and sensible as they wrote a legal brief listing the colonists' grievances. *When in the course of human events, it becomes necessary for one people to dissolve the political bands which have connected them with another...*

Thomas Jefferson (1743–1826) is a representation of the ideal, cultured **man of the Enlightenment** who did many things well. He was an excellent violinist, singer and dancer. Fluent in six languages, he translated several books, including the Bible, from the original languages. An accomplished architect and inventor, he applied science to farming and was knowledgeable about meteorology. His personal library became the nucleus for the Library of Congress.

While serving as Ambassador to France, Jefferson invited **Jean-Antoine Houdon** (1741–1828), a great **sculptor** of the time, to the United States. Houdon, who was known for his accurate portrayals, sculpted George Washington at Mt. Vernon.

*Houdon's images of Franklin, Jefferson and Washington
are found on the fifty-cent piece, nickel and quarter.*

The Minuet in the United States of America

In the colonies, manners and customs, including music, were modeled after English society.

- A Governor's Ball was held on the King's birthday. Guests were often entertained with elaborate feasting and dancing, especially on Southern plantations. Daughters, servants and slaves provided the music.

- By 1700, music instructors and dancing masters, usually with a European background, were common.

- By 1750, concerts, operas, and musical evenings in homes or assembly halls were frequent in larger American cities. Immediately following many concerts, the instrumentalists would provide music for a formal ball, traditionally opened with a minuet.

- **George Washington** (1732–1799) enjoyed music, the theater, and especially dancing.

---

[10]Joseph Machlis & Kristine Forney, *The Enjoyment of Music* (New York: W. W. Norton & Co., 1995), 227.

George Washington (1788) by Jean-Antoine Houdon. Richmond, Virginia, Capitol Building

Minuet and Trio

The most common form of the minuet in the Classical period was the **minuet and trio.** The minuet and trio was the form frequently used for the **third movement of multi-movement classical forms** (like sonata, symphony or string quartet). In performance both sections of the minuet are repeated, followed by both sections of the trio. After the trio, the minuet is traditionally played again without repeating the sections.

■ Minuet and trio **similarities:** usually in binary form and about the same length.

■ Minuet and trio **differences:** keys, theme, character and texture of the music.

(This is the form for the *Minuet Danced before Mrs. Washington* on the following page.)

┌—**Minuet**—┐ ┌—**Trio**——┐ ┌**Minuet Repeated**┐
(sections not repeated)

Sections: ‖: A :‖: B :‖: C :‖: D :‖ A ‖ B ‖

La Dance

Two engravings by Daniel Chodowiecki

The engraving on the right illustrates the graceful dignity expected of 18th-century men and women in contrast to the affected and inappropriate gestures and stance of the couple on the left.

The French musician and dancing master, **Pierre Landrin Duport**, performed and taught in Philadelphia. This minuet is from a collection of dance tunes in the Library of Congress. It was performed *"by two young ladies in the presence of Mrs. Washington in 1792."*[11]

An engraving of Martha Washington

Minuet Danced before Mrs. Washington

Pierre Landrin Duport
(1762–1841)

Track 4

[11] Carl Engel, introduction to *Music from the Days of George Washington* (Washington, DC: George Washington Bicentennial Commission, 1931), viii.

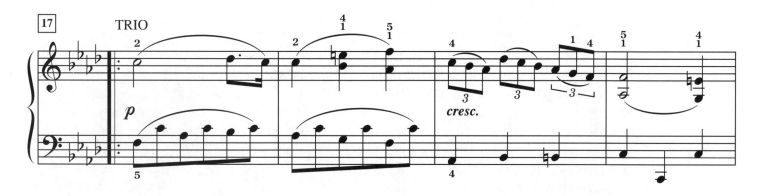

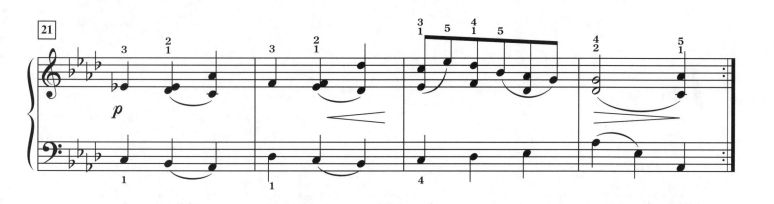

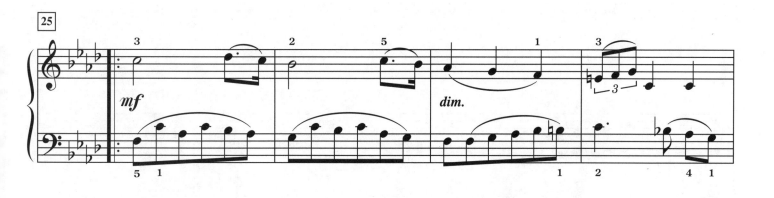

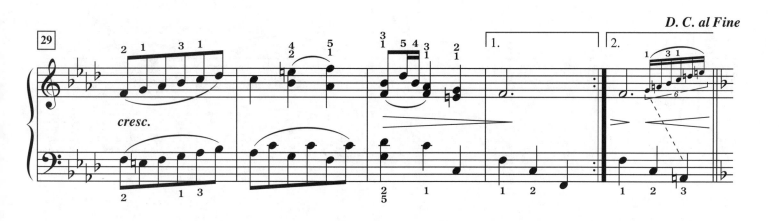

Scherzo and Trio

By the mid-18th century, composers sometimes **replaced the minuet and trio with a scherzo and trio.** Ludwig van Beethoven used the title "scherzo" instead of "minuet" in most of his works. The form remained essentially the same, but scherzos were **faster** than minuets and, since scherzo literally means **joke**, the character of the music was more **humorous** and, at times, boisterous.

Carl Maria von Weber was a composer, conductor, music critic and one of the first to use the piano in a dramatic way in his compositions and as a virtuoso performer. Greatly influenced by Beethoven, Weber was a leader in the transition from Classical- to Romantic-style piano music.

Scherzo

Carl Maria von Weber
(1786–1826)

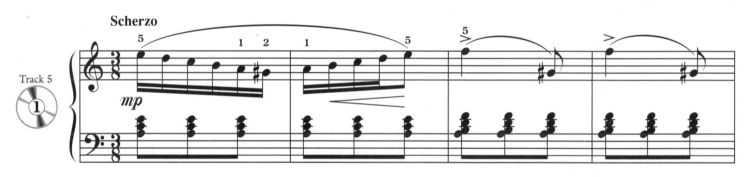

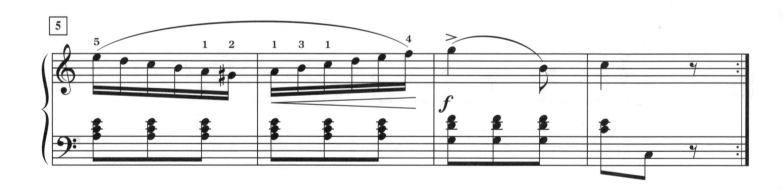

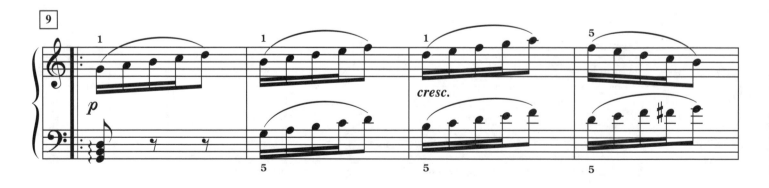

Court of King Frederick the Great

Frederick II, King of Prussia (1712–1786), laid the foundation for modern Germany by expanding the power, territory and influence of Prussia during his 46-year reign. He did this through his military brilliance and his intellectual and artistic abilities and interests.

- Almost immediately after becoming King, he went to war, gained control over Silesia, and in later years won other territories as well.

- Frederick saw himself as the Greek philosopher, Plato's (ca. 428–347 B.C.) **enlightened philosopher-king,** allowing freedom of speech and religion, and establishing cultural institutions such as a science academy and the Berlin Opera.

- His Court in Berlin was French in language, manners, furnishings and architecture, yet he gathered the finest thinkers, artists, dancers and musicians from all of Europe. He practiced the flute four times a day and considered musical activities an escape from state duties. Arising at 4 a.m., most days ended with a late dinner and an evening concert where he performed some of the 300 flute concertos he knew.

Carl Philipp Emanuel Bach (1714–1788), Johann Sebastian's second and most famous son, was the principal keyboard player at the Court of Frederick the Great for nearly 30 years. C.P.E. Bach made a distinction between his father's **"learned,"** more contrapuntal style of composition, and the newer *style galant* favored by composers of his generation. *Galant* music, usually performed in small, intimate settings, had a freer texture and was frequently written for female amateurs.

Flute Concerto at Sans Souci *by Adolf von Menzel.*
King Frederick the Great playing the flute
accompanied by C.P.E. Bach at the keyboard.

Characteristics of *Style Galant* or Classical Style Music

One aspect of the newer *style galant,* also characteristic of Classical-style music, is a **balanced phrase structure** with a melody divided into **short two- to four-measure segments** set off by cadences. The following *Allegro in G Major* has many two-measure melodic segments that begin with a pick-up note.

---

[12] Giles Macdonogh, *Frederick the Great* (New York: St. Martin's Press, 2000), jacket.

Allegro in G Major

Carl Philipp Emanuel Bach
(1714–1788)

While employed at the Court in Berlin, **C.P.E. Bach** published many keyboard works for the general public. Among them were *"musical portraits of several young ladies known to him in the form of short keyboard pieces…people…have assured me that their temperament has been expressed."*[13] A **harmonized melody** predominates and is another characteristic of *style galant* and Classical-style music.

$\mathcal{L}$a Caroline

Carl Philipp Emanuel Bach
(1714–1788)

Allegro mà con tenerezza
(Quickly, but with tender emotion)

Track 7

(a) The editor suggests playing a **Schneller** in this piece.

[13] Hans-Günter Ottenberg, *Carl Philipp Emanuel Bach*, quoting from the introduction to the first issue dated Nov. 22, 1760 (New York: Oxford University Press, 1991), 102.

Georg Anton Benda played violin in Frederick the Great's orchestra. He traveled to Italy, France and Austria and composed operas and church music as well as many songs and keyboard pieces. This **one-movement sonatina** (small sonata) is in binary form, similar to the sonatas of Domenico Scarlatti (1685–1757). One **rhythmic motive** dominates.

Sonatina in D Major

Georg Anton Benda
(1722–1795)

"More can be lost by poor fingering than can be replaced by all conceivable artistry and good taste."

C.P.E. Bach[14]

C.P.E. Bach published keyboard music in a wide variety of styles. This *Presto in C Minor* is from a 1768 collection called *Short and Easy Piano Pieces with Varied Repetitions*. In this piece, the **A¹** section (measures 17–32) is a **varied repetition** of the **A** section (measures 1–16). Likewise, **B¹** (measures 57–72) is a varied repetition of **B** (measures 33–56).

Presto in C Minor

Carl Philipp Emanuel Bach
(1714–1788)
Wq. 114/3

[14]Kathleen Kimball, ed., *The Music Lover's Quotation Book* (Toronto: Sound and Vision, 1990), 86.

> *"[A clavichord]...is tender and responsive to your soul's every inspiration,...here you will find your heart's soundboard...in the contact with those wonderful strings and caressing keys."*
>
> Christian Schubart (1739–1791), German composer and poet[15]

Empfindsamkeit (Sensitive/Sentimental Style)

In North Germany in the mid-1700s, there was a movement to create sensitive, emotional expression or "true and natural" feelings in music. It was a reaction to more rational *"melodies that say nothing and merely tickle the ear;"*[16] and of *"music that falls on the ear and fills it up, but leaves the heart empty."*[17]

- The leading exponent of this style in keyboard music was C.P.E. Bach who believed the purpose of music was to *"move the heart..."*[18] He wanted to move quickly from one emotion to another without speech. To accomplish this, he used dissonance, sudden changes in keys, dynamics and harmonies; contrasting themes, and sections in free rhythm, which, in his lifetime, many found to be bizarre. His music has an improvisatory quality with sections of instrumental recitatives and cadenza-like passages. This is evident in his **fantasias**.

A large clavichord, popular in 18th-century Germany

To My Clavier
Thou faithful stringed array,
Echo my sighing soul!...
Fond strings, obey my hand,
Help me my pain withstand—[19]

Eighteenth-century German songbooks had many poems similar to this in various musical settings.

- C.P.E. Bach's favorite keyboard instrument for personal use was the **clavichord**, and he had a large one built to his specifications.

- The clavichord's simple construction (a metal tangent on the end of the key) made it inexpensive. It was especially popular with German families.

- The tone was small (about ppp to p), but was sensitive to changes in touch. It was called *"a consolation in grief and a friend in joy."* [20]

[15] *New Grove Dictionary of Music and Musicians*, s.v. "Clavichord" (London: Macmillan, 1980), vol. 4, 466.

[16] Ibid., s.v. "Empfindsamkeit," vol. 6, 157.

[17] Ibid., quoting C.P.E. Bach, 158.

[18] Ottenberg, *C.P.E. Bach*, 3.

[19] Arthur Loesser, *Men, Women & Pianos* (New York: Simon and Schuster, 1954), 61.

[20] Dr. Mark Zilberquit, *The Book of the Piano*, trans. by Yuri S. Shirokov (Neptune, NJ: Paganiniana Publications, Inc., 1987), 15.

"Keyboardists whose chief asset is mere technique...overwhelm our hearing without satisfying it and stun the mind without moving it..."

C.P.E. Bach[21]

Fantasia in G Major

Carl Philipp Emanuel Bach
(1714–1788)

[21] Kimball, *The Music Lover's Quotation Book,* 61.

Wilhelm Friedemann Bach (1710–1784) was the oldest, and perhaps the most gifted, son of J. S. Bach. At a young age he assisted his father with rehearsals, taught and copied music. He completed his education in math, philosophy and law at the University in Leipzig.

- Known as an organ virtuoso, he became the Court organist in Dresden. Later employed by the city of Halle, he abruptly left without notice. His final years were spent erratically teaching, composing and giving concerts. He died in poverty.

"Learned" and New Style Elements Combined

Many composers during the late 18th century shifted between **"learned" (old) and new style elements**, sometimes within the same work. W. F. Bach was extremely successful in this.

- The following *Aria* opens with a balanced phrase structure divided into **short segments**. **Melody** is prominent **in a light texture** typical of the newer *style galant*.

- The second (**B**) section is in a more **"learned" or contrapuntal style** used by his father and other Baroque composers. Measure 19 begins a passage with a **motive and two sequences** where both hands are equal in importance.

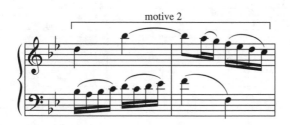

- The *Polonaise in D Minor* (page 36) is an example of the *empfindsamkeit,* or **sensitive style** so associated with his brother, C.P.E. Bach.

This aria combines new *style galant* elements with more "learned" or contrapuntal style.
See page 33 for musical examples from this piece.

ria

Wilhelm Friedemann Bach
(1710–1784)

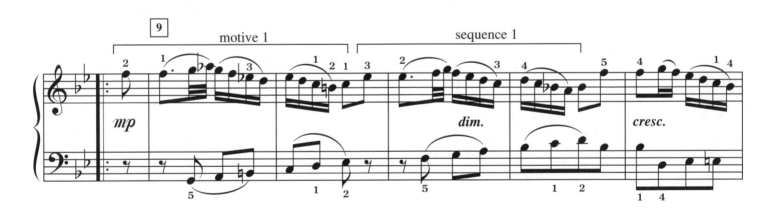

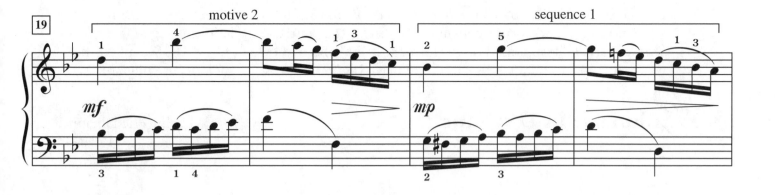

This is from a set of 12 polonaises by **W. F. Bach.** Sighing chromaticism, daring harmonies, and abrupt dynamic shifts show the **sensitive style** in this regal dance form. An early edition, based on performances by **Johann Forkel** (1749–1818), stated that polonaises in minor keys should be played *adagio* with slow, melodic appoggiaturas.

Polonaise in D Minor

Wilhelm Friedemann Bach
(1710–1784)

"The Italians exalt music; the French enliven it; the Germans strive after it; and the English pay for it well."
Johann Mattheson (1681–1764), German composer, critic, theorist[22]

London, a Musical Hub

In the late 18th century, London was the leading city in **public musical life.** Music at the Court was less important, and few aristocratic families in England had household musicians. Music was needed for outdoor parties, indoor gatherings, amateur music societies, operas, and public concert halls. Native and continental musicians filled the demand.

Music Publishing in London

- Having **musical skills** was seen as a necessary **social accomplishment**, creating **upper- and middle-class amateurs**[23] who needed "easy" printed music to sing and play, affordable instruments and music lessons.

- Modern music publishing was established in London around 1700 and soon became a significant industry. Professional critics wrote concert reviews in journals, instruction books were published with helpful advice for amateurs, and music catalogs advertised Sonatas, Lessons, Methods and Collections (for harpsichord or piano) by leading composers of the day.

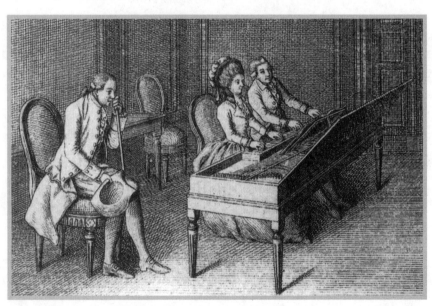

Title page for Six Sonatas for Two Persons at One Clavier.

A duet being played on a square piano.

1781 engraving by Johann August Rosmaesler for Franz Seydelmann

Keyboard Sonata and Sonatina

The term **sonata** had different meanings at different time periods but always referred to an instrumental piece that became associated with the keyboard. When first used in 1669, **sonatina**, a small sonata, was linked with amateurs and teaching.

- **Some 18th-century sonatas** were played by keyboard virtuosos in concerts, but most were intended for domestic use, sometimes with an accompanying instrumentalist.

- By 1750, **sonata** referred most often to a **three-movement** plan of **fast–slow–fast**. In England, sonatas were sometimes called **lessons**, implying self-improvement.

---

[22] Derek Watson, ed. introduction and selection, *Dictionary of Musical Quotations* (Ware Hertfordshire: Cumberland House, Wordsworth Editions Ltd., 1994), 79.

[23] Derived from the Latin word "to love," a musical amateur (lover of music), refers to one pursuing it as a pastime rather than a profession.

William Duncombe was an English harpsichordist, pianist and organist. This sonatina is from his *First Book of Progressive Lessons for the Harpsichord and Piano-forte* published in London around 1780.

Sonatina in C Major

William Duncombe
18th century

Intrada

In most published versions of the *Fanfare Minuet,* measures 17–19 are exactly the same as measures 1–3. The added notes in measures 17–19 are in Duncombe's original edition and help to build excitement in the final fanfare.

Fanfare Minuet

The Hunt
Gigue

Allegro

(a) The editor suggests that the appoggiaturas be played before the beat.

"His [Johann Christian Bach] keyboard works were such 'as ladies can execute with little trouble.'"

Dr. Charles Burney (1726–1814), 18th-century music historian[24]

Piano Manufacturing in London

- ◼ In 1760, a group of German instrument makers immigrated to London, including **Johann Zumpe** (1726–1790). He built a successful business manufacturing square pianos for the home, and *"he could not make them fast enough to gratify the craving of the public,"* according to Dr. Burney.[25]

- ◼ In 1768, Johann Christian Bach performed a **public solo piano concert** on a **five-octave Zumpe** giving it public credibility and exposure.

- ◼ By 1780, there were two types of grand pianos dominating Europe: the English (Broadwood) and the German or Viennese (Stein). Each model had a unique mechanical action.

Johann Christian Bach (1735–1782), the youngest son of Johann Sebastian and Anna Magdalena Bach, was first taught music by his father and then by his older brother, Carl Philipp Emanuel, in Berlin. Known as a keyboard virtuoso, J.C. went to Italy to study opera, composed church music there, and became the Milan Cathedral organist.

- ◼ Success with his operas in Turin and Naples led him to London in 1762 to conduct Italian opera. Appointed Music Master to the Queen in London, he performed, taught, published Lessons and Sonatas, and organized public concerts.

- ◼ Making London his home, he had great influence on many contemporary musicians, including the eight-year-old Mozart who spent a year there.

Zumpe square piano, manufactured between 176 and 1765

A Sunday Concert at the Home of Charles Burney *(a satirical engraving). Dr. Burney, at front right, could not stop gossiping, even during the concert.*

Dr. Burney traveled Europe and in 1771 published The Present State of Music in France and Italy, a General History. *Other regions were covered in 1773 and 1775 volumes.*

[24] James Galway, *Music in Time* (New York: Harry N. Abrams, Inc., 1983), 131.
[25] David Crombie, *Piano, A Photographic History* (San Francisco: GPI Books, 1995), 18.

This toccata is from *Introduction to the Piano, a Method for the Forte-Piano*, co-authored by **J. C. Bach** and **Francesco Pasquale Ricci** (1732–1817). First published in Paris in 1786, *Introduction* contains 100 pieces that emphasize technical skills. **One motive and its sequential patterns** dominate this toccata. The motive enters a second time in measure 11, this time in the left hand together with a new right-hand voice. This complete pattern is then sequenced several times.

occata

Johann Christian Bach
(1735–1782)

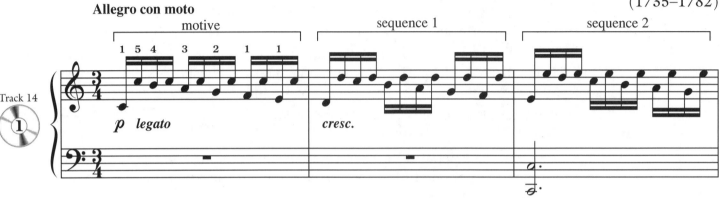

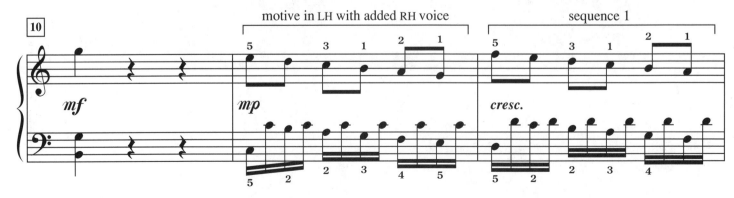

Taught mainly by his father, Johann Sebastian, **Johann Christoph Friedrich Bach** (1732–1795) took his first position as a court musician in Bückenburg around the time of his father's death. After becoming *Konzertmeister* there, he composed, produced and conducted many oratorios, cantatas, symphonies, operas and chamber music.

- Taking a leave from the Court in 1778, he and his son, **Wilhelm Friedrich Ernst** (1759–1845), traveled to London to visit J.C.F's brother Johann Christian. While there, J.C.F. purchased a pianoforte and a great deal of music. They also attended many musical events, including J.C. Bach's new opera. J.C.F. returned home, leaving his son in London to continue his musical training.

- An outstanding virtuoso, most of J.C.F. Bach's published keyboard pieces were short and in *style galant* with a few in the "expressive" style.

Anglaise

The **anglaise** (English dance) was a term used on the Continent to describe all dance music thought to have originated in England. Late in Louis XIV's (1638–1715) reign, French dancing masters imported English **country dances** to enliven court balls.

Originating in English villages, it was a simpler, more "natural," yet energetic dance. Second in popularity only to the minuet during the 18th century, it was slightly modified in Louis XIV's Court. There it was known as **contredanse** (counter/opposite) since couples faced each other, rather than the King, as they danced in lines.

Country Dance *by William Hogarth (1697–1764).*
Hogarth was a popular painter and engraver who satirized many aspects of English society in his art.

Anglaise

Johann Christoph Friedrich Bach
(1732–1795)

Track 15

"Let others make war for a throne—You, happy Austria, marry..."

Anonymous poem[26]

Musical Austria

The German **Habsburgs** were the most powerful royal family of Europe, controlling vast territories of land acquired through battles and shrewd marriages. During the 13th century, they gained control of Austria and ruled until the end of World War I (1918).

- **Leopold I** (1640–1705) married a Spanish princess. His daughter, **Maria Theresa** (1717–1780) married the French Duke of Lorraine (1708–1765) and they had 16 children. A son, **Joseph II** (1741–1790), married an Italian princess, and daughter **Marie-Antoinette** (1755–1793) married Louis XVI (1754–1793) of France.

- Also **patrons of the arts,** the Habsburgs imported Italian operas as well as other foreign artists, composers and performers. Many were **accomplished musicians** themselves with Leopold I a highly skilled composer, conductor and performer.

Photo: Kunsthistorisches Museum

Emperor Joseph II of Austria with two of his sisters. He was a good singer, viola, cello and keyboard player, and often accompanied performances at Court.

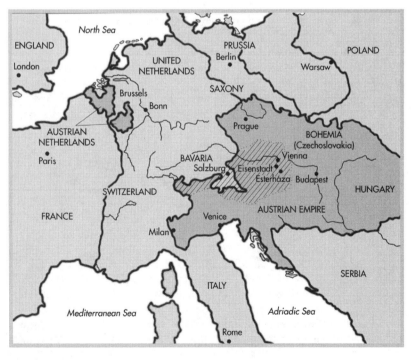

The Austrian Empire around 1780

Austria Today

- The size of the **Austrian Empire** helped it develop a unique musical style during the Classical period. It became the **melting pot** for the Germanic culture of central Europe, the music and vocal style of Northern Italy, the cultural and folk elements of Hungary and the Slavs, and the brilliant wind playing of Bohemia (today's Czech Republic) with touches of French and Spanish ingredients.

[26]Richard Rickett, *A Brief Survey of Austrian History* (Vienna: Georg Prachner Verlag, 1966), 27.

Carl Ditters von Dittersdorf's father was a costumer at the Imperial Court in Vienna. Having grown up in that environment, Carl was privileged with an excellent education. He composed all forms of music and his over 100 symphonies have been compared to Haydn's. He wrote **20 English dances** for keyboard.

English Dance

Carl Ditters von Dittersdorf
(1739–1799)

Track 16

(a) The editor suggests that the appoggiatura be played before the beat.

Johann Baptist Vanhal, although born in Bohemia, studied music in Vienna with Carl Ditters von Dittersdorf and established himself there as a teacher and composer. He is known to have played in a string quartet with Dittersdorf, Haydn and Mozart.

Allegretto in A Major

Johann Baptist Vanhal (1739–1813)
Op. 41, No. 12

ienna, Musical Capital of Europe

Capital of the Austrian Empire, **Vienna** was also the **musical capital of Europe** during the Classical period. Around 1750 it had a French emperor (husband of **Maria Theresa**), an Italian Court poet and composer, performances of French-style operas and ballets, and concerts by Belgian, German and Austrian instrumentalists, making it a **cosmopolitan city**.

Maria Theresa began her reign in 1740. A trained singer with a great love for the theater, she soon divided her group of about 130 musicians into two smaller groups; one performed sacred music and the other operas. The Court eventually took over the management of Vienna's two leading theaters.

When theaters closed during Lent, public concerts were allowed. **Public subscriptions** were frequently sold in advance to cover expenses for the musician who organized the event. People of all social classes attended the theater, operas, ballets and public concerts.

Nobility from the entire Empire had palaces in Vienna as well as other residences and estates in the various regions. One estimate was that 8,000 aristocrats were residing in Vienna in the 1780s since all spent part of each year there. Great rivalry developed among the aristocrats for the finest orchestras and musicians.

Engraving by Karl Schütz (1785) of St. Michael's Square in Vienna showing the Burgtheater, where many of Mozart's operas, symphonies and piano concertos were premiered.

---

[27] Neil Butterworth, *Haydn, Illustrated Lives of the Great Composers* (New York: Omnibus Press, 1987), 73.

Patronage and the "Viennese Masters"

Music was very important for status to all social classes. Wealthy aristocrats hired musicians as **part of their household** and it was common to see advertisements in Viennese newspapers for servants who could also play a musical instrument. Although there was some economic security, a professional musician's rank was little better than that of a servant.

Some patrons (frequently middle-class) would **commission a favorite composer** to write a work for a specific event, or hire musicians for a **single performance**. Other aristocrats organized concerts and paid leading musicians to participate.

- **Franz Joseph Haydn** spent over 30 years as Director of Court Music for the Esterházy family He had a restrictive contract, wore a servant's uniform, and said that he sat at their dinner table "below the salt." Since ambassadors, royalty, and even the Empress Maria Theresa visited the Esterházy estates, Haydn eventually became very famous and financially independent.

- **Wolfgang Amadeus Mozart** left his position at the Court in Salzburg and never secured another Court position. As a freelance musician, his income came from performing, publishing, fulfilling commissions, and giving lessons. Although he had some success with his operas and his subscription concert series (where he performed his piano concertos), he died in poverty.

- **Ludwig van Beethoven** had a contract with three Viennese noblemen who agreed to pay him a salary to remain in Vienna and compose. He was not seen as a servant, but was recognized and rewarded because of his extraordinary musical gifts. By the early 1800s, he was offered more commissions than he could accept. He boasted that he could set a high price and get it.

The Palace at Eszterháza, Hungary,
where Haydn was employed.

"There was no one near me to upset or torment me, so I was forced to become original."

Haydn on his years at the Eszterháza Palace[28]

Franz Joseph Haydn

Haydn was highly respected and his music was known throughout Europe during his lifetime. He stated that what he had accomplished was a result of great need.

- At age six, he was sent from his small Austrian town to live with his cousin who was a musician and teacher. After two years of intense study, he was accepted as a choirboy at St. Stephen's Cathedral in Vienna.

- There he was educated and instructed in singing, violin and keyboard. During his nine years in the choir, Haydn said he had two lessons in theory and none in composition. He taught himself by carefully studying the music he heard and sang.

- Dismissed when his voice changed, he was without money, a job or a place to live. He taught and accompanied, played the violin, composed for chamber music evenings in aristocratic homes, and for a time was a servant to an opera composer.

- He gradually became known in musical circles, and in 1761 was hired to conduct the orchestra of the Hungarian Prince Paul Esterházy (1711–1762).

- At this time the Esterházy family owned about 25 palaces and castles and one and a half million acres of land. A choir, orchestra, military band and actors were part of the household staff. Haydn was in charge of all musical instruments and musicians and was to compose and rehearse music desired for any occasion.

- Prince Nicholas Esterházy (1714–1790) spent the equivalent of four million dollars building the Esterháza Palace that he patterned after Versailles. Designed for entertaining, the opera house seated 400, there were two concert halls, a marionette theater and 126 guest rooms. The family employed Haydn until his death.

*Engraving of Franz Joseph Haydn (1792)
by Luigi Schiavotti*

---

[28] Alan Kendall, *The Chronicle of Classical Music* (London: Thames and Hudson Ltd., 1994), 99.

This *Presto in G Major* shows the optimistic spirit common in **Haydn's** music. The opening section is based upon a rhythmic motive that is expanded and then repeated. The G minor section (measures 25–48) has a contrasting texture.

This same music is found **twice in his 62 keyboard sonatas**. It is the **last** of a three-movement sonata (H. XVI/G1; L. 4), and the **first** of another three-movement sonata (H. XVI/11; L. 5).

*P*resto in G Major

Franz Joseph Haydn
(1732–1809)

Minuet in C Minor

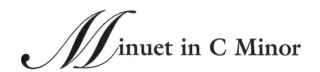

Franz Joseph Haydn
(1732–1809)

ⓐ The editor suggests that the appoggiaturas be played before the beat.

Wolfgang Amadeus Mozart

- Mozart was a genius from birth, playing keyboard melodies at age 3, performing publicly and composing by age 5. At age 6, he was taken on his first concert tour where he performed with his older sister, **Nannerl** (1751–1829).

- A report of a performance at age 7 tells he *"could play in an adult manner, improvise in various styles, accompany at sight, play with a cloth covering the keyboard, add a bass to a given theme, and name any note that was sounded."*[30]

- By age 8 he had performed at the Courts in Bavaria and Salzburg, for Maria Theresa in Vienna, Louis XV (1710–1744) at Versailles, and for George III (1738–1820) in London. In 1770, he was honored by Pope Clement XIV (1705–1774) in Rome. He was able to assimilate everything from his extensive travels to France, Italy and England into his compositions.

- At a program in Italy (prepared by professional musicians) he performed as soloist in a piano concerto followed by a solo sonata, both of which he read at sight. He then added variations and transposed the sonata. Next he was given words for an aria that he instantly composed and sang while accompanying himself. He was given a theme and improvised both a sonata and fugue on it. He also played violin in a trio and conducted one of his symphonies. Mozart was 14.

- He and Franz Joseph Haydn became friends, and although Mozart was much younger, the two exchanged ideas and influenced each other in their musical compositions.

A 1763 engraving of Mozart at the keyboard with his father, Leopold (1719–1787), playing the violin and his sister, Nannerl, singing.

[29]Crofton & Fraser, *Musical Quotations*, 97.

[30]*New Grove Dictionary, s.v.* "Mozart, Wolfgang Amadeus," vol. 12, 681.

Composed while on tour in Zurich when Mozart was 10 years old, he never gave this piece a title. On that trip, he also performed in Amsterdam, Brussels, Paris and Munich.

𝒦lavierstücke in F Major

Wolfgang Amadeus Mozart
(1756–1791)
K. 33B

"Everything comes from the theme."
Franz Joseph Haydn[31]

Mozart originally wrote this piece for wind instruments. Published before 1800, it is believed to be his own keyboard arrangement. The lyric expressiveness of the opening theme shows Mozart's great **melodic gifts**.

Andante in C Major

Wolfgang Amadeus Mozart
(1756–1791)

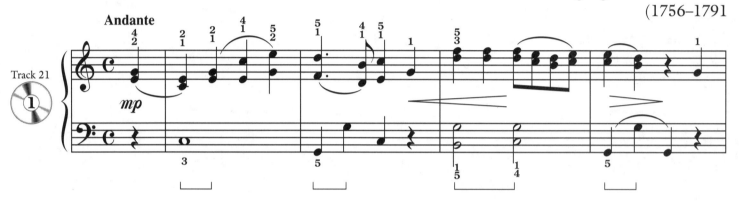

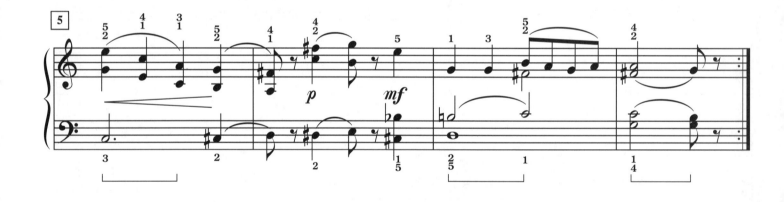

---

[31] Charles Rosen, *The Sonata Forms* (New York: W. W. Norton & Co., 1988), 177.

This was written as a joke for Barbara von Ployer, one of Mozart's students. It is believed to be a parody of the opening of his *Concerto in G Major*, K. 453, which he composed for her.

$\mathcal{M}$arche funèbre del Signor Maestro Contrapunto
(Funeral March for Masterful Mr. Counterpoint)

Wolfgang Amadeus Mozart
(1756–1791)
K. 453a

"Prince, what you are, you are by the accident of birth; what I am, I am of myself. There...will be thousands of princes. There is only one Beethoven."

Letter to Prince Lichnowsky, 1806[32]

Ludwig van Beethoven

With the piano greatly improved, a public that wanted to hear and play music, and a wide variety of established instrumental forms (that unlimited by words were capable of expressing an infinite range of emotions), the stage was set for **Beethoven**.

- Ludwig was the third generation of court musicians in **Bonn**. His father, a singer, saw that he had good musical training, and by age 11, he was an assistant to the Court organist. By 13, he had published works.

- Beethoven made a brief visit to Vienna where it is believed **he met Mozart** and had a few lessons with him. In 1792, Beethoven returned to Vienna to study with Haydn and spent the rest of his life there. When he left Bonn, Count Waldstein said, *"You shall receive Mozart's spirit from Haydn's hands."* [33]

- From Vienna, Beethoven toured and performed as a piano virtuoso in palaces of the aristocracy, private homes, and in public concerts. He published works by subscription and was at the height of success when he began to go deaf. His increasing deafness forced him to stop performing and to compose full-time.

- He was kindhearted, but frank to the point of rudeness. He had an uncontrollable temper, and such sloppy personal habits that he lived 80 different places in Vienna. His genius ultimately overcame his eccentric and erratic behavior.

Photo: AKG London

When they met in Vienna, Mozart reportedly said, "Keep an eye on that young man [Beethoven]. Someday he will make a big splash in the world." [34]

[32] Crofton & Fraser, *Musical Quotations*, 15.

[33] *New Grove Dictionary*, s.v. "Beethoven, Ludwig van," vol. 2, 357.

[34] Kimball, *The Music Lover's Quotation Book*, 40.

"When writing for the public, one undoubtedly writes most beautifully—and also rapidly."

Ludwig van Beethoven[35]

Ludwig van Beethoven composed this waltz in 1824 for publication in an album of dance pieces. It shows his interest in the unique sound and color possibilities of the piano and his use of unusual pedal effects.

Waltz in E-flat Major

Ludwig van Beethoven
(1770–1827)
WoO 84

[35] Crofton & Fraser, *Musical Quotations*, 15.

64 *The Classical Piano, Part 1*

ⓐ Beethoven indicated to depress the pedal here but did not say where to lift it. The editor suggests holding the damper pedal down, without change, throughout the section to give the effect of a bagpipe.

ⓑ The editor suggests that the appoggiaturas be played before the beat.

This folkdance is the **theme** from a set of four variations for **piano with an added flute or violin**. The **accompanied sonata,** extremely popular during the 18th century, was *"essentially an amateur domestic medium, designed for lady pianists of moderate skill and gentlemen string-players of yet more slender accomplishment."*[36]

*L*ändler
(Tyrolean Air)

Ludwig van Beethoven
(1770–1827)
Op. 107, No. 1

Track 24

[36] James Parakilas and others, *Piano Roles,* quoting from "Concert Life in London" (New Haven: Yale University Press, 1999), 26.

Part 2

The Influence of 16 Great Classical Composers

Sonata Form

Some scholars mark the beginning of the Classical period around 1780 with the solo keyboard sonatas of Franz Joseph Haydn (1732–1809) and Wolfgang Amadeus Mozart (1756–1791), culminating in the 32 sonatas of Ludwig van Beethoven (1770–1827).

A **sonata**[1] at this time was understood to be a **multi-movement instrumental** work (usually three or four movements) with the **movements varied in tempo, style,** and **form** according to their placement in the cycle (first, second, last).

The most common forms[2] (and character) for each movement are as follows:

First Movement	*Forms:* Sonata-Allegro (see below), Theme and Variations *Character:* Dramatic
Second Movement	*Forms:* Three-part song form (A B A), Sonata-Allegro, Theme and Variations, Minuet and Trio *Character:* Slow and lyrical
Third Movement (frequently omitted)	*Forms:* Minuet and Trio, Scherzo and Trio *Character:* Dancelike
Last Movement	*Forms:* Rondo—A form where a main theme (A) alternates with one or more secondary themes (B or C). The most common pattern is A B A C A. Sonata-Allegro, Theme and Variations, Minuet and Trio *Character:* "Happy ending"[3]

Sonata-Allegro (First Movement) Form

Exposition…*where* the material for the piece is first stated or "exposed."

Dramatic in character	**Theme 1** (in the home key) leads to a Bridge section that prepares for **Theme 2**
More lyric in character	**Theme 2** (in a different key)

Development…*where* the material from the Exposition is "developed" or transformed.

Previously presented themes or fragments are changed, tension is built and resolution occurs with the recapitulation.

Recapitulation…*where* the material from the Exposition is "restated" with some changes.

Dramatic in character	**Theme 1** (in the home key) leads to a Bridge section that prepares for **Theme 2**
More lyric in character	**Theme 2** (this time also in the home key)

---

[1] The musical forms of sonatas and sonatinas (little sonatas) are essentially identical. Sonatinas are usually shorter and easier to perform.

[2] All the forms listed on this page can be found throughout *The Classical Piano* book.

[3] Joseph Machlis and Kristine Forney, *The Enjoyment of Music* (New York: W.W. Norton & Company, 1999), 234.

[Czerny was] *"warmer than all his compositions."*
Frédéric Chopin (1810–1849)[4]

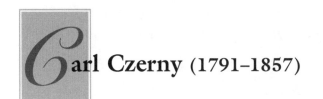

Carl Czerny (1791–1857)

Carl Czerny was one of the most industrious, prolific and influential pianists of all time. As a pupil of Ludwig van Beethoven (1770–1827) and the only teacher of Franz Liszt (1811–1886), he occupies a unique place in the development of piano playing and teaching.

- Born near Prague, Czerny was taught the works of Johann Sebastian Bach (1685–1750), Wolfgang Amadeus Mozart (1756–1791) and Muzio Clementi (1752–1832) beginning at age three by his father. At ten he began **piano lessons with Ludwig van Beethoven** in Vienna and remained in that city most of his life.

- A wonderful pianist known for interpreting Beethoven's works, he played them all from memory. He stopped performing publicly at a young age and devoted himself to teaching, composing and writing. His commentary on Beethoven's music (based on Beethoven's performances and their lessons together) is of great value today.

- He wrote compositions in all forms, but his legacy is the **thousands of etudes** (studies) in his 861 piano opuses that explore every aspect of piano technique. Pianist **Ferruccio Busoni** (1866–1924) stated he could always hear in a pianist's technique if his education had been *"with or without Czerny."* [5]

Czerny, the Teacher

Czerny wrote a survey of music history, treatises on composition, improvisation, piano playing and teaching, and became the most famous piano teacher in Europe. Considered by many to be the **founder of modern piano technique**, he insisted upon absolute accuracy and naturalness of technique and interpretation. He emphasized beautiful tone, assigned daily scale practice, and it was said he spent more lesson time on interpretation and artistic problems than on technical exercises.

His pupils include:

Beethoven's nephew,
Carl van Beethoven (1806–1858),
Stephen Heller (1813–1888),
Sigismond Thalberg (1812–1871),
Theodor Kullak (1818–1882),
Theodor Leschetizky (1830–1915),
and Franz Liszt (1811–1886).

Carl Czerny
Lithograph by Engleman,
published by Maurice Schlesinger, Paris

---

[4] *New Grove Dictionary of Music and Musicians,* s.v. "Carl Czerny" (London: Macmillan, 1980).
[5] Isidor Philipp, "Czerny: Master of Masters," *Etude Magazine* (September 1939): 563.

This charming *Allegretto in C Major* is in two-part **binary form**. Typical of the form, it cadences on a **V** chord (G major) at the end of Part 1, ending in C major in Part 2. The entire piece is based on one short motive.

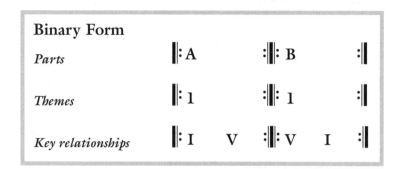

Binary Form			
Parts	‖: A	:‖: B	:‖
Themes	‖: 1	:‖: 1	:‖
Key relationships	‖: I V	:‖: V I	:‖

$\mathcal{A}$llegretto in C Major

Carl Czerny (1791–1857)
Op. 792, No. 8

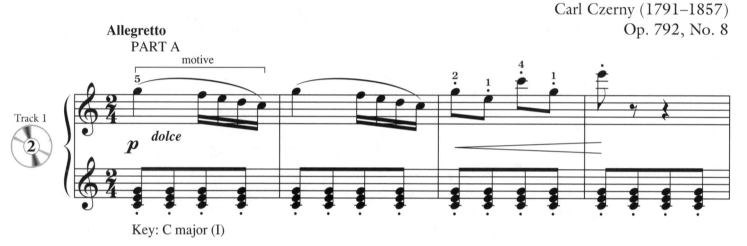

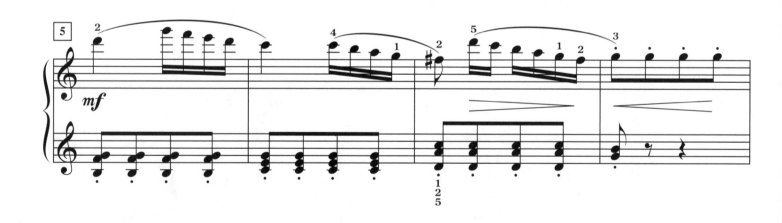

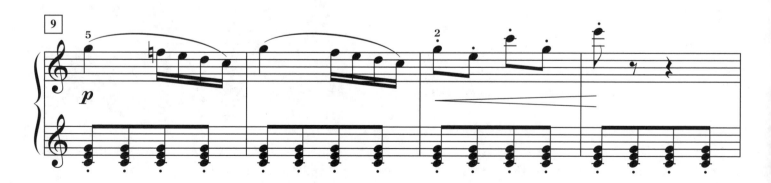

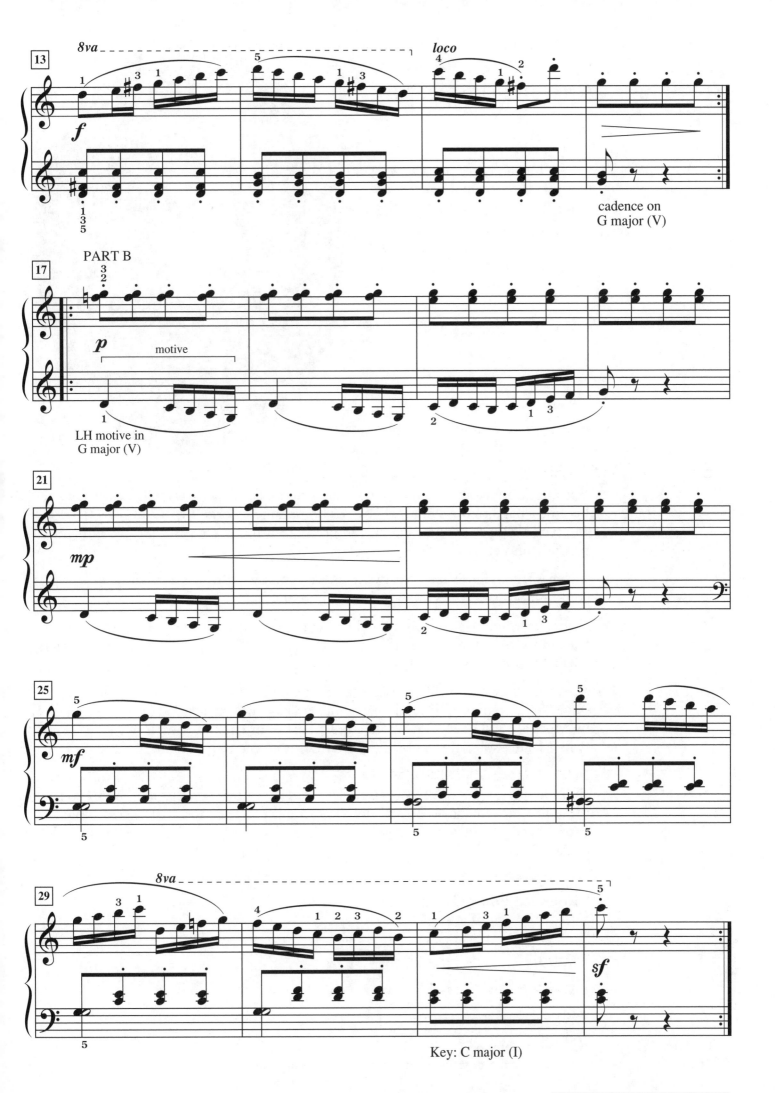

cadence on
G major (V)

PART B

LH motive in
G major (V)

Key: C major (I)

*T*homas Attwood (1765–1838)

"He [Thomas Attwood] shows more of my style than any [student] I ever had; and I predict, that he will prove [to be] a solid musician."
Wolfgang Amadeus Mozart (1756–1791)[6]

Portrait of Thomas Attwood by an unknown artist
Royal College of Music, London

Thomas Attwood, an English composer, was closely associated with the British Royal Family throughout his life.

- Born in London, at age nine he became a choirboy at the Royal Chapel. Later, he became a page to the Prince of Wales who became George IV (1762–1830). Impressed with Attwood's talent, the Prince sent him to the European continent to study music.

- Thomas studied in Naples for two years and then went to Vienna where he was a composition student of Mozart for one and one-half years.

- Upon returning to England, he held several different positions. He was music teacher to the Duchess of York and the Princess of Wales, composer to the Royal Chapel and organist at St. Paul's Cathedral.

- Active in all aspects of London's musical life, he composed over 30 works for the stage, was a founder of the Philharmonic Society (where he conducted a symphony by Mozart every year), and wrote a great deal of organ and church music. When Felix Mendelssohn (1809–1847) visited London, the two became friends.

- In 1795 Attwood published a set of *Easy Progressive Lessons Fingered for Young Beginners on the PianoForte or Harpsichord*. The following **sonatina**[7] (short sonata) is the first movement of the second piece from the set, and is in **rounded binary form**, where the opening theme and the home key both return in the second half of Part B.

Rounded Binary Form

Parts	‖: A	:‖: B		:‖
Themes	‖: 1	:‖: 2	1	:‖
Key relationships	‖: I (C major)	:‖: V[7](G major feeling)	I (C major)	:‖

---

[6] *New Grove Dictionary*, s.v. "Thomas Attwood."

[7] In general, sonatinas have short development sections, and are used as teaching material.

Sonatina No. 2 in C Major
(first movement)

Thomas Attwood
(1765–1838)

"This Kind of Music is not...calculated so much for public Entertainment, as for private Amusement. It is rather like a Conversation among Friends."

18th-century advertisement for sonatas[8]

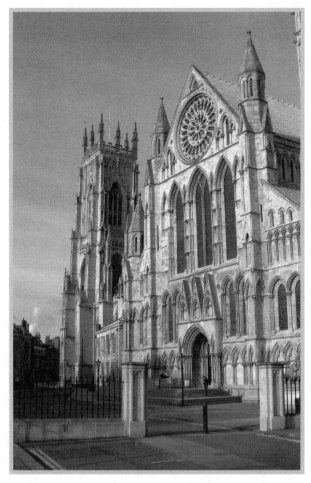

York Minster Cathedral, located in York, England, is the largest Gothic cathedral in northern Europe. Begun in 1220 and completed in 1470, its nave is the second highest in England.

Matthew Camidge (1764–1844)

Four members of the **Camidge** family were organists and composers in direct succession at York Minster Cathedral (York, England) for over 100 years. **Matthew Camidge** held the position from 1799–1842.

- **John Camidge** (ca. 1734–1803), the father of Matthew, was thought to have studied with George Frideric Handel (1685–1759) in London before returning to York. It is believed that he began the tradition of singing excerpts from Handel's *Messiah* at Christmas and Easter services instead of using anthems.

- Matthew was trained in London as a choirboy at the Royal Chapel, but returned to York where he assisted his father and succeeded him upon his retirement. Matthew became well known throughout northern England as an organist, conductor of oratorios, and as a director of large music festivals.

- He published 25 sonatas and sonatinas and, as was customary, most had violin and cello accompaniments. The *Sonatina in G Major* is in **sonata-allegro form**. Typical of this form, the dramatic tension created in the **development section** is resolved at the **recapitulation**, when the opening theme and the home key both return.

Sonata-allegro form developed out of Baroque binary form and is a flexible framework of three sections (exposition, development and recapitulation) in a two-part structure.

Sonata-Allegro Form				
Part	A		B	
Section	Exposition		Development	Recapitulation
Theme	1	2		1 2
Key relationship	I (G major)	V (D major)	V (D major)	I (G major)

[8] *New Grove Dictionary*, s.v. "Sonata."

$\int$onatina in G Major
(first movement)

Allegro moderato
PART A
Exposition

Matthew Camidge
(1764–1844)

Track 3

The Classical Piano, Part 2 **75**

PART B
Development

Key: D major (V)

Domenico Cimarosa (1749–1801)

Domenico Cimarosa was one of the most prolific composers of his time writing more than 80 operas, dozens of choral works and more than 50 piano sonatas.

- Born into a poor family in Naples, Italy, Cimarosa was educated by monks in exchange for his widowed mother doing their laundry. Accepted at the Conservatorio di Santa Maria di Loreto at age 11, he studied keyboard instruments, violin, singing and composition there.

- His first opera was successfully premiered during the 1772 Carnival season in Naples. In the next 10 years he wrote more than 40 operas, which were performed in many cities including Rome, Venice and Vienna. He was Court Composer to Catherine the Great (1729–1796) in St. Petersburg, Russia. He later had a similar appointment in Vienna.

- His most successful comic opera, *The Secret Marriage*, was first presented in Vienna in 1792, two months after Mozart's death. The Emperor liked it so much that he ordered dinner for the entire cast and demanded a repeat of the entire opera (the longest encore in history). He gave Cimarosa a gift of money equal to about two years the salary he had paid Mozart, plus a diamond-studded snuffbox.

- Franz Joseph Haydn (1732–1809) conducted 13 of Cimarosa's operas at Eszterháza.

Domenico Cimarosa
Museo di San Martino, Naples, Italy

"Only Mozart and Cimarosa can portray the rarest shades of emotion in music."
Beyle Stendhal (1783–1842), French writer[9]

[9] John Amis & Michael Rose, *Words About Music* (New York: Paragon House, 1983), 227.

Cimarosa's keyboard sonatas show variety in his use of forms. The following
Sonata in G Major is in **sonata-allegro form**. However, the **recapitulation section**
omits the first theme, beginning with the second theme in the home key of G major.

*S*onata No. 6 in G Major
(first movement)

Domenico Cimarosa
(1749–1801)

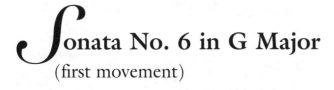

"He [Haydn] alone has the secret of making me smile, and touching me to the bottom of my soul."
Wolfgang Amadeus Mozart (1756–1791)[10]

A performance of Haydn's oratorio, The Creation, *at the University of Vienna on his 76th birthday in 1808. Beethoven, Hummel and Salieri were all present. Haydn was so weak he had to be carried into the hall. It was his last public appearance. Aquatint by Balthasar Wigand (1771–1846).*

Franz Joseph Haydn (1732–1809)

During the long life of **Franz Joseph Haydn**, musical style changed from the late Baroque to mature Classical. The piano overtook the harpsichord in popularity, and a more precise meaning for the word **sonata**[11] developed. Haydn's musical evolution is shown in the more than 60 keyboard sonatas written throughout his life.

- Employed by the wealthy Hungarian Esterházy family for over 30 years, Haydn was required to compose church music, operas, and all types of instrumental music. His patron allowed him to publish his compositions; after 1779, many of his keyboard sonatas were published in Vienna, Paris, London and other cities.

- Most of his early sonatas are titled **divertimento** or **partita** (terms used at this time for multi-movement instrumental works of a light, entertaining nature). When Haydn used this title, they all had a **fast-minuet-fast** sequence of movements.

- The length of Haydn's sonatas vary, having two, three and four movements. After meeting Mozart and exchanging ideas, Haydn's **development sections** become more complex and the **recapitulation** became more of a "reinterpretation" of the **exposition**. Scholars consider his final three sonatas, written during his second trip to London in 1794–1795, to be masterpieces.

- Despite the great diversity in the sonatas (and all his music) his unique imagination, craftsmanship, natural charm and humor are always evident.

---

[10] <http://www.composers.net/database/h/Haydn.html>
[11] A multi-movement instrumental form with formal implications for each movement (see page 68).

This **three-movement sonata** may have been written as early as the 1750s when most of Haydn's income came from teaching piano, and it is thought to have been composed for his students. The first and last movements are both in **sonata-allegro form**. The first movement is more typical of a **sonatina** since the sections are very brief.

$\mathcal{S}$onata (Divertimento) in C Major

Franz Joseph Haydn (1732–1809)
Hob. XVI/7; L. 2

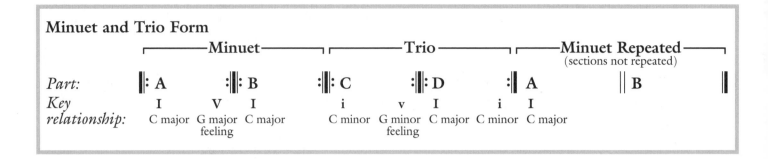

Minuet and Trio Form

	Minuet			Trio		Minuet Repeated (sections not repeated)	
Part:	‖: A	:‖: B	:‖: C	:‖: D	:‖ A	‖ B	‖
Key relationship:	I	V I	i	v I	i I		
	C major	G major feeling / C major	C minor	G minor feeling / C major	C minor / C major		

Minuet

Binary Form

Allegretto

PART A

Track 6 ②

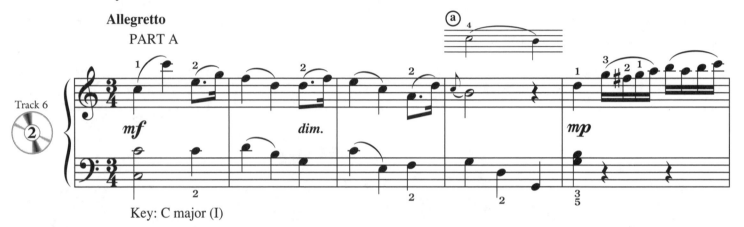

mf   *dim.*   *mp*

Key: C major (I)

cresc.   PART B   *mf*   *dim.*

V (G-major feeling)

mp   *cresc.*   *Fine*

Key: C major (I)

ⓐ When an appoggiatura is followed by a rest in Haydn's music, the second note is played in place of the rest.

Trio

Rounded Binary Form

Key: C minor (i)
(parallel minor)

V (G-minor feeling)

Key: C major (I)

Key: C minor (i)

Minuet da Capo

Finale

Allegro

Exposition

Theme 1

Key: C major (I)

Theme 2

Key: G major (V)

ⓐ The editor suggests playing a *Schneller* here and in measure 48 (see page 10).

Friedrich Kuhlau
Engraving by Emil Barentzen

*[Kuhlau,] "Sultan [Ruler] of the Classical Sonatina.
They are always written in a serious and noble style."*
Carl Weitzmann (1808–1880),
German writer and composer[12]

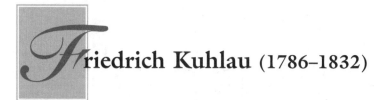

*F*riedrich Kuhlau (1786–1832)

German born **Friedrich Kuhlau** spent most of his life in Denmark where he had great influence on Danish music and composers. Today he is known for both his piano sonatinas and his flute music. He has been called the "Beethoven for the flute."

- **Friedrich Kuhlau** was born into a family of German military bandsmen. When he was about 10 years old he fell and, as a result of the accident, lost his right eye. During his recovery, he began studying music. Around 1802 he settled in Hamburg where he continued music studies, performed piano recitals, and where his works were first published.

- When Napoleon's army invaded the city, he escaped to Denmark and established himself as a musician in Copenhagen. He became a Danish citizen, was named Royal Court Composer, taught, published, and became widely known as a concert pianist. His operas (frequently on Danish subjects and using Danish folk tunes) were very popular.

- Beethoven presented him with a portrait inscribed, *"To my friend, Kuhlau"* after they spent an evening in Vienna improvising canons for each other.

- His major income came from publications of entertaining piano duets, pieces for flute and piano, and piano sonatinas, rondos and variations. His piano works have become standard repertoire for the developing pianist, especially as preparation for the Beethoven sonatas.

Theme and variations, one of the oldest musical forms, has been used by composers from the 10th through 20th centuries. The theme is generally played at the beginning and is changed in subsequent statements either melodically, harmonically or rhythmically.

---

[12] Gorm Busk, Charles, K. Moss, English ed., *Friedrich Daniel Rudolph Kuhlau,*
<http://classicalmus.hispeed.com/articles/kuhlau.html>.

Variations on an Austrian Folk Song

Friedrich Kuhlau (1786–1832)
Op. 42, No. 1

Variation III 25

29

Variation IV 33

37

Variation V

Variation VI

Carl Philipp Emanuel Bach (1714–1788)

In the late-18th century, **Carl Philipp Emanuel Bach** was known as the "Great" Bach, being more famous than his father, Johann Sebastian, or his musical brothers. He helped to make his father's name and works more widely known, even though he wrote in a different style.

▣ As the second son from J. S. Bach's first marriage, C. P. E. Bach was trained by, and later assisted, his father. He also met the many famous European musicians who visited their home. His formal schooling was at the Thomasschule in Leipzig followed by seven years studying law at the University of Leipzig.

▣ In 1738, C. P. E. was hired on the staff of the crown prince and future king, Frederick II (1712–1786) of Prussia. As principal keyboard player for the Court in Berlin, his salary was one-tenth that of the leading opera singer.

▣ After almost 30 years, he left to become Music Director for the city of Hamburg, succeeding his godfather, Georg Philipp Telemann (1681–1767). With duties similar to J. S. Bach's in Leipzig, C. P. E. Bach taught musical and nonmusical subjects at the boys' choir school, and was responsible for all music at five city churches (about 200 performances a year).

Keyboard Music

Many of his keyboard works were published "for ladies" and "Connoisseurs and Amateurs." His more than 90 keyboard sonatas contributed to the development of idiomatic piano style, and all three "Viennese Masters" (Haydn, Mozart and Beethoven) acknowledged his influence.

In 1775 he published *Essay on the True Art of Playing Keyboard Instruments,* an important source on 18th-century keyboard technique, fingering, and ornamentation. Today it is studied more than his compositions.

Carl Philipp Emanuel Bach (center), Pastor Sturm (right) and the artist, Andreas Stöttrup (pen and ink drawing with wash)

Copyright: Hamburger Kunsthalle
Photographer: Elke Walford, Hamburg

[13] Derek Watson, ed. intro. and selection, *Dictionary of Musical Quotations* (Ware Hertfordshire: Cumberland House, Wordsworth Editions Ltd., 1994), 108.

Published in 1753 as *18 Probestücke* (18 test-pieces in the form of 6 sonatas), this is the first movement of the sixth *Sonata in F Minor*, and is in **rounded binary form**. Its dramatic character makes it an example of the ***Sturm und Drang*** (Storm and Stress) movement associated with C. P. E. Bach.

onata in F Minor
(first movement)

Carl Philipp Emanuel Bach
(1714–1788)

Key: C minor
(V minor)

Theme 1

Key: F minor

*"He could replace our father better
than all the rest of us put together."*
C. P. E. Bach (1714–1788)[14]

Wilhelm Friedemann Bach (1710–1784)

Wilhelm Friedemann Bach was the oldest son from J. S. Bach's first marriage. The *Little Keyboard Book for Wilhelm Friedemann Bach* was presented to him by his father when he was 10. It includes the *Inventions, Sinfonias, Little Preludes,* and part of the *Well-Tempered Clavier, Book 1,* a testament to the young boy's ability.

- W. F. Bach also studied violin, and was an outstanding student at the University of Leipzig. In 1729, he visited George Frideric Handel in Halle, Germany, and invited him to come to Leipzig to meet his father, but Handel and J. S. Bach never met.

- When W. F. Bach was 23 years old, he was appointed organist at St. Sophia Church in Dresden. It was said his playing was so superior that no other candidate had a chance. He had high social status at that time, since many considered him to be the finest organist in Germany. He also composed a wide variety of music there.

- He then moved to Halle where he was organist at a large church and also conducted an orchestra. In 1764, W. F. Bach resigned, claiming he was not sufficiently recognized. He never secured another position.

- For the rest of his life, he gave organ recitals, taught, composed music to sell, and even sold many of his father's manuscripts. He made barely enough money to live and left his wife and daughter in poverty.

- Some scholars believe he was his father's most gifted and favorite child. He used more counterpoint than his brothers in a basically homophonic texture. His music has beautiful melodies, daring harmonies, and very emotional and expressive qualities.

[14] *Wilhelm Friedemann Bach,* <http://www.composers.net/database/b/BachWF.html>

Allegro in A Major

Wilhelm Friedemann Bach
(1710–1784)

Johann Christian Bach (1735–1782)

"My brother [C. P. E. Bach] lives to compose while I compose to live; he works for others, I work for myself."

J. C. Bach[15]

Portrait of Johann Christian Bach by Thomas Gainsborough (1727–1788)

The youngest son of Anna Magdalena and J. S. Bach, **Johann Christian** spent most of his life in London where he met and influenced young Mozart. Highly respected in his lifetime, his music was seldom performed after his death.

- When J. C. Bach's father died in 1750, Wilhelm Friedemann took him to Berlin to live with his half brother, C. P. E. Bach. J. C. Bach later traveled to Italy where he became known as an organist and composer of church music and operas.

- In 1762, he went to London to compose operas for the King's Theater and, except for brief trips abroad, remained there. He organized concerts (where he also conducted and performed), wrote and published many works, became music teacher to the Royal Family and performed regularly when the Queen entertained.

- As a keyboard performer and teacher his entire life, his keyboard music has beautiful melodies, balanced phrases, and slow harmonic rhythms. It is an example of *style galant* (gallant style) with its sophistication and charm. Some writers have described it as, *"a little bit empty"* (emotionally).

- The Mozart family spent about a year in London when Wolfgang was eight. He performed for the King and Queen sitting on J. C. Bach's knee as they played duets and alternated on the same keyboard. Leopold Mozart (1719–1787) held up J. C. Bach's music to his son as a model and told him to write with J. C. Bach's *"natural, easy and flowing style."* Upon hearing of J. C. Bach's death, W. A. Mozart commented, *"What a loss to the musical world."* [16]

[15] Norman Lebrecht, *The Book of Musical Anecdotes* (New York: Macmillan, Inc., 1984), 49.
[16] Maynard Solomon, *Mozart* (New York: HarperCollins Pub., 1996), 317.

Risoluto

Johann Christian Bach
(1735–1782)

Risoluto vif et decidé
(Decisively, fast and
with determination)

Track 11

J. C. Bach and **Francesco Pasquale Ricci** (1732–1817) co-authored *Introduction to the Piano, a Method for the Forte-Piano* (1786). It opens with information necessary for a beginning keyboard student to know—terms, forms, musical signs and ornaments. This is followed by 100 progressive pieces in various styles and forms designed for musical and technical development to promote artistry. *Risoluto* (page 101) and *Largo Affannoso* are from this method.

*L*argo Affannoso

Johann Christian Bach
(1735–1782)

(a) J. C. Bach wrote the direction *a mezzo voce* (half voice) at the beginning of the piece.
(b) The editor suggests playing the appoggiaturas in measures 3, 9 and 14 very quickly, on the beat.

"The student was required to draw forth the tone out the instrument by means of an elastic touch and to coax sounds out of it, not as is so common today, to pound them out."

Carl Loewe (1796–1869), pupil of Türk[17]

Daniel Gottlob Türk (1750–1813)

Teacher, theorist, and composer, **Daniel Gottlob Türk** is known for his theoretical writings. Beethoven used his *Clavierschule* (The School of Keyboard Playing) in his teaching, and it is an important source today for late-18th-century keyboard performance style.

- Daniel was first trained in music by his father, an instrumentalist for a German court. At the University of Leipzig, Türk had keyboard lessons with a pupil of J. S. Bach and studied C. P. E. Bach's *Essay on the True Art of Playing Keyboard Instruments*.

- At 24, he moved to Halle and became a leader in that city's musical life. There he held church positions (succeeding W. F. Bach in one) and taught general subjects at the Lutheran school. As Professor of Music at Halle University, he conducted many performances, as well as lecturing in theory, composition and music history. During this time, he composed many works and published 15 collections of piano music.

Clavierschule

It was common for prominent 18th-century composers, performers and teachers to publish instruction manuals. Other professionals, as well as **musical dilettantes** (aristocracy and nobility) and middle-class **amateurs** used them. Intended to supplement lessons, they included information on how to develop technical skills, how to practice, how to gain musical taste and understanding, as well as exercises and pieces.

Türk's *Clavierschule,* published in 1789, was in print over 50 years. Türk discusses characteristics of a good teacher, as well as fingering, ornamentation, improvisation, articulation, and how to stir emotion in students and listeners. He included his own music and a list, in order of difficulty, of sonatas and sonatinas available at that time.

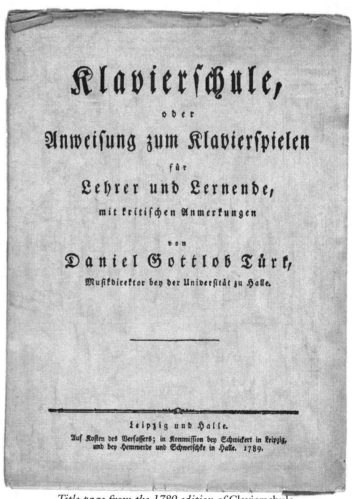

Title page from the 1789 edition of Clavierschule

---

[17] Türk, *Clavierschule,* intro. by Raymond H. Haagh, Xv.

In 1792 and 1795, Türk published sets of piano pieces to be used along with his *Clavierschule*, which was used by most piano teachers at that time. He included titles to guide the student's imagination or to show the technical purpose.

Solemn and Moving

Daniel Gottlob Türk
(1750–1813)

$\mathcal{T}$hose Broken Octaves!

Daniel Gottlob Türk
(1750–1813)

Track 14

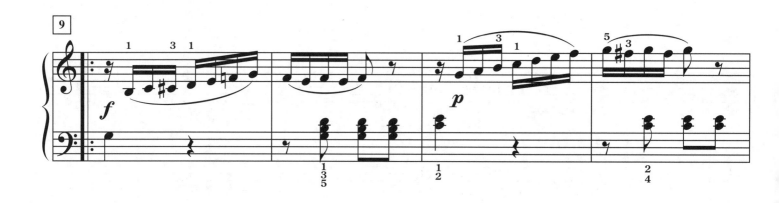

Mercure de France (French newspaper), 1784[18]

Maria Theresia von Paradis (1759–1824)

By age 16, **Maria Theresia von Paradis** had performed as a singer and virtuoso keyboard player in Vienna. A successful European concert tour followed. She later taught piano, voice, and theory in a music school that she helped found.

- Daughter of the Imperial Secretary and Councillor to the Viennese Court, Paradis was named after the Austrian Empress, Maria Theresa (1717–1780). She developed normally until age two, when she awoke one day with convulsions and eye twitching, and became totally blind.

- Because of her great talent, the Empress paid for her to have the best education possible, including composition and voice lessons with Antonio Salieri (1750–1825) who wrote an organ concerto for her. Mozart and Haydn both wrote piano concertos for her. One of her teachers invented a pegboard to help her compose.

An etching by Faustine Parmantié (1784)

- Her concerts were extremely popular with the public. It was said she could play over 60 concertos from memory. Her mother accompanied her on a three-year concert tour where she met the Mozarts in Salzburg, C. P. E. Bach in Hamburg, performed for George III (1738–1820) and accompanied the Prince of Wales in London, and appeared 14 times in Paris. She also performed in Frankfurt, Brussels, Amsterdam and Prague.

- After the age of 30, she did less performing, devoting her major energies to composing and teaching.

---

[18] Carol Neuls-Bates, ed., *Women in Music* (New York: Harper & Row, 1982), 85–86.

A **sicilienne** was a dance originating in Sicily in moderately slow 6/8 or 12/8 time with the character of a **pastorale**, suggestive of an idyllic rural scene. A tender lyrical melody, reminiscent of a shepherd's pipe (flute), with a chordal accompaniment is typical. Sicilienne-like movements appeared frequently in 18th-century instrumental music, sometimes as the slow movement of a sonata. There is frequent use of the rhythmic pattern:

Sicilienne

Attributed to
Maria Theresia von Paradis
(1759–1824)

Track 15

(a) Originally for violin and piano, the editor arranged this for piano solo.
(b) The editor suggests playing the appoggiaturas very quickly, before the beat.

An 18th-century portrait of Mozart

AKG London

Wolfgang Amadeus Mozart (1756–1791)

Acclaimed during his childhood by the crowned heads of Europe as a brilliant prodigy, he was widely known as a composer and virtuoso all his life. Legends have grown around his death and unknown burial site, but the universal recognition of **Wolfgang Amadeus Mozart's** genius has not ceased.

- Playing keyboard melodies at three, composing minuets at five, a symphony at eight and an opera at twelve, Mozart could apparently do everything without being taught. His fame was spread through Europe by extensive concert tours with his sister, **Nannerl** (1751–1829).

- As an adult, Mozart settled in Vienna and earned money from teaching, performing and commissions. In 1787, Emperor Joseph II (1741–1790) gave him a small salary to compose dance music for court balls. *"Too much for what I do, too little for what I could do,"*[20] Mozart supposedly said. Plagued with financial difficulties most of his adult life, he was buried in a common grave with others at an undiscovered location.

- With over 600 compositions in all forms, his greatest works are considered to be his symphonies, piano concertos, and operas. Mozart's complex operatic characters communicate emotions beyond the words. The music displays people with contradictions, sorrow, self-importance, dignity—a full range of emotions.

- Much of his keyboard music was written for his own performance. There are 18 piano sonatas, but most consider him to be the **creator of the classic concerto**; his **piano concertos** are considered his keyboard masterpieces. They have been compared to his operas with their lyric beauty, continuous conversation and dramatic interplay between the piano soloist and orchestra. Mozart's joyous spirit is personified in the lively finales.

[19] Neil Butterworth, *The Illustrated Lives of the Great Composers: Haydn* (New York: Omnibus Press, 1987), 71.

[20] Philip G. Downs, *Classical Music* (New York: W. W. Norton & Company, 1992), 492.

Written in 1790, Mozart may have intended to use this lovely *Andantino* for a set of variations. The theme is by the Viennese opera composer Christoph Willibald Gluck (1714–1787).

Andantino in E-flat Major

Wolfgang Amadeus Mozart (1756–1791)
K. 236 (588b)

This rondo was originally written for stringed instruments and horns and is the last movement of a six-movement suite. Mozart composed it for a wealthy family in Salzburg in 1781. A **rondo form** alternates one theme with other material and is frequently used for final movements. This rondo alternates only two themes: **A A B A B A coda.**

Rondo in C Major

Wolfgang Amadeus Mozart
(1756–1791)

ⓐ The editor suggests playing the appoggiaturas very quickly: begin the single appoggiaturas in measures 3, 7, 11, 15, 23 and 31–33 before the beat and the appoggiatura groups in measures 13 and 21 *on* the beat (as indicated by the dashed lines between the hands).

"...with one foot in classicism and one in romanticism, taking the best of each [he fused] them into that higher something we have called "Beethovenism."
Robert Haven Schauffler (1879–1964), author, lecturer and musicologist[23]

Ludwig van Beethoven (1770–1827)

A revolutionary by nature with a powerful personality, **Ludwig van Beethoven's** struggle with deafness was directed to creative energy that transformed the sonata framework, which was established by Haydn and Mozart, into symphonies, chamber music, piano sonatas and concertos of deeply felt personal expression. It is estimated that 10,000 people attended his funeral in Vienna.

- Before the late-18th century, music was primarily for religious services and entertainment for royalty and the public. Emotions expressed were common to humans, and not personal, because audiences were best pleased by music that was not too difficult and not too serious.

- At the beginning of his career, few recognized Beethoven's genius as a composer. He was better known as a pianist. Since his early teachers were musicians first, and not professional pianists, he was basically a self-taught pianist. His performances were a phenomenon of *"fiery expression,"* with wrong notes, broken hammers and strings, and an emotional intensity that overpowered audiences, especially in his improvisations.

- He once performed his C major *Piano Concerto No. 1,* Op. 15, in the key of B major because the piano was out of tune by a half tone. His **five piano concertos** are among the best selling classical recordings of all time. His **32 piano sonatas** are a landmark in the history of music and have been nicknamed the pianists' *New Testament* (the *Old Testament* being J. S. Bach's *Well-Tempered Clavier*).

© Erich Lessing / Art Resource, New York

Masqued Ball in the Redoutensaal by Joseph Schütz on occasion of the Congress in Vienna, with the performance of Beethoven's Seventh Symphony and his composition "Wellington's Victory in the Battle of Vittoria." Color print located in the Historisches Museum der Stadt Wien, Vienna, Austria

[23] *The Beethoven Companion,* s.v. "A Summing Up," by Robert Haven Schauffler (Garden City, NY: Doubleday & Company, Inc., 1972), 1,199.

Minuet in E-flat Major

Ludwig van Beethoven (1770–1827)
WoO 82

Track 18

Johann Nepomuk Hummel (1778–1837)

Considered to be one of the greatest composers and pianists of his time, **Johann Nepomuk Hummel** impacted future pianists through his teaching (Carl Czerny was his student) and with his piano method in which he wrote that *"every trill should begin with the note itself, and not the note above, unless the contrary be expressly indicated.*"[22]

- Hummel was such a prodigy that when he was seven, Mozart accepted him as a student, taught him free of charge, and allowed him to live with the Mozart family in Vienna for two years. At 10, Hummel's father took him on a four-year concert tour that included a two-year stay in London. While there, he studied with Clementi and expanded his piano technique.

- After returning to Vienna, he spent several years studying composition (with Haydn, Salieri and others), composing, teaching, and performing as a conductor and pianist. Beethoven was his greatest pianistic rival, and many preferred Hummel.

- In 1804, he succeeded Haydn as Director of Court Music for the Esterházy family, but his contract was terminated after seven years. In 1818, he became Music Director to the Court in Weimar where he was in charge of the court theater and all other musical performances.

- For many years there was friction between Hummel and Beethoven, but Hummel traveled to visit the dying Beethoven and was a pallbearer at his funeral. At Beethoven's request, Hummel improvised on themes from the dead composer's works at the memorial concert.

- Hummel's three-volume piano method, *The Complete Theoretical and Practical Course of Instructions on the Art of Playing the Piano Forte* (1828), was said to have sold thousands of copies within days of its publication. The following *Scherzo in A Major* is among its 2,000 musical examples.

- Hummel composed an enormous amount of music in his lifetime including operas, masses, chamber music, orchestral works, concertos and numerous piano solos. Scholars see him as linking the late-Classical styles of Clementi and Mozart with the Romantic styles of Schubert, Mendelssohn, Chopin, Liszt and Schumann.

---

[21] Marion Barnum, "Hummel—One of the Great Pianists of the Past," *Clavier Magazine* (March–April 1975): 15.
[22] Harold C. Schonberg, *The Great Pianists* (New York: Simon and Schuster, 1966), 110.

Scherzo in A Major

Johann Nepomuk Hummel
(1778–1837)

Alexander Reinagle (ca. 1750–1809)

One of the many musicians who immigrated to America after the American Revolution, **Alexander Reinagle** was influential in setting high standards by performing music of J. C. Bach, Haydn, Handel, Johann Baptist Vanhal (1739–1813) and other European composers in the concerts he organized.

- Reinagle grew up in Scotland, taught in Glasgow and had keyboard works published there before moving to London. He visited C. P. E. Bach in Hamburg, Germany, and also traveled to Portugal, taught in Lisbon, and performed for the Royal Family there.

- Arriving in New York City in 1786, he settled in Philadelphia where he revived a city concert series and became its manager. George Washington (1732–1799) attended concerts where Reinagle performed during the Constitutional Convention. Washington later engaged him to teach music to his adopted daughter, Nelly Custis (1779–1852).

- Reinagle taught Philadelphia's leading families, and helped form a theatrical company that also performed in other cities. He oversaw the construction of a theater, advertised as one of the seven wonders of the New World. He also managed the theater, and composed, arranged, performed and conducted whatever was needed. Hundreds of different types of works for the stage were performed there, including operas. *"He became the acknowledged leader of music in this city; and in those days that was equivalent to making the statement apply to the whole country."*[25]

- Several of his keyboard works were published in Philadelphia including *Scots Tunes with Variations*, which includes *Steer Her Up and Had Her Gawn*. First published in Glasgow, the 1787 edition was the earliest-known commercially available keyboard work published in America. The melodies were native Scottish melodies and Robert Burns (1759–1796) wrote verses on many of the tunes.

Alexander Reinagle, from a drawing by Joseph Muller

[24] Anne McClenny Krauss, "More Music by Reinagle," *Clavier Magazine* (May–June 1976): 18.
[25] Joseph Francis Ambrose Jackson, *Encyclopedia of Philadelphia* (Harrisburg, PA, 1933), IV: 951.

Steer Her Up and Had Her Gawn

Alexander Reinagle
(ca.1750–1809)

Variation 1

Variation 2

Variation 3

Variation 4

"When the composer leaves the staccato and legato to the performer's taste, [no articulation is marked in score]...adhere to the legato, reserving the staccato...to set off the higher beauty of the legato... Keep down the first key until the next has been struck."

Muzio Clementi[26]

Muzio Clementi (1752–1832)

Portrait engraving by Thomas Hardy (1840–1928)

Muzio Clementi was a virtuoso pianist, a sought-after teacher, prolific composer, music publisher and piano manufacturer. Called the **father of modern piano playing**, he regarded legato playing to be the norm unless otherwise indicated (in contrast to the detached style of playing advocated by C. P. E. Bach and Daniel Gottlob Türk).

- Born in Rome, Italy, he was so gifted that he had an organ position by age nine. A visiting aristocrat took him to England and supervised the boy's education and training. Clementi became well known in London as a pianist, conductor and composer.

- Foreign tours included performances in St. Petersburg and Moscow, for Queen Marie Antoinette (1755–1793) in Paris, and a pianistic "duel" with Mozart before Emperor Josef II (1741–1790) in Vienna. Mozart and Clementi first played their own compositions and then improvised on a theme. Mozart reported that the court piano was out of tune and three keys were stuck, but the Emperor assured them it didn't matter.

- Clementi said of Mozart, *"Until then I had never heard anyone play with such spirit and grace."*[27] Mozart wrote his sister, *"What he [Clementi] really does well are his passages in thirds, but he sweated over them day and night in London."*[28] Scholars believe that Mozart's playing commanded respect, while Clementi had a more bravura technique of fast thirds, sixths, octaves and arpeggios, as well as showmanship that thrilled audiences.

- After he returned to London, it was said Clementi's fee for piano teaching was twice all others, and he demanded payment in advance for 20 lessons. A composer of symphonies and over 100 piano sonatas, his lasting influence on generations of pianists rests primarily with his Op. 36 sonatinas, the etudes in the *Gradus ad Parnassum* and his *Introduction to the Art of Playing on the Piano Forte*.

- A shrewd businessman who was extremely wealthy in his lifetime, he negotiated an exclusive contract to publish some of Beethoven's works at his London publishing house. Clementi was so esteemed that he was buried in Westminster Abbey.

---

[26] Reginald Gerig, *Famous Pianists & Their Technique* (Bridgeport, CT: Robert B. Luce, Inc., 1985), 60.

[27] *New Grove Dictionary*, s.v. "Clementi, Muzio."

[28] Schonberg, *Great Pianists*, 48.

A **monferrina** is a country dance in 6/8 time originating in the Piedmont region of northern Italy. It became fashionable in England around 1800. This is one of the few "recreational" pieces (so popular with pianists at this time) that Clementi wrote. He composed 24 waltzes (with optional triangle and tambourine parts) and 18 monferrinas.

Monferrina

Muzio Clementi (1752–1832)
Op. 49, No. 7

(a) The editor suggests playing the appoggiaturas very quickly, before the beat.